SEVEN

SIGNIFICANCES

OF

THE CROSS

By

Andrew Allans Mutambo.

Unless otherwise noted, all scripture quotations are from the original King James Version of the Bible.

To order copies online visit:
http://www.andrewmutambo.com
Or by mail contact:
Andrew Allans Mutambo
P.O BOX 22292
Kampala, Uganda.
U.S Line: 1-804-601-0394.
Uganda line: +256-77-240-4389

Email: andymutts@gmail.com

Rivendell Publishing
www.rivendellpublishing.com

Dedication

This book is dedicated to the King of Glory for His grace and wisdom to write this manuscript. I pray that every reader will be inspired and equipped to embrace the truths herein.

Acknowledgements

My family and fellow Pastors in Revived Glory Church, thank you for your continuous encouragement, love, prayers, and time to pursue my authorial dream. To my Church family, my sincere gratitude for your love, support and patience during the times of separation and study in the course of writing my books. Your love and prayers are always appreciated.

Table of Contents

Preface

The Christian Cross, seen as a representation of the instrument of the crucifixion of Jesus Christ, is the best-known religious symbol of Christianity. It is related to the crucifix (a cross that includes a usually three-dimensional representation of Jesus' body) and to the more general family of cross symbols.

The cross-shaped sign, represented in its simplest form by a crossing of two lines at right angles, greatly antedates, in both East and West, the introduction of Christianity. It goes back to a very remote period of human civilization. It is supposed to have been used not just for its ornamental value, but also with religious significance.

It may have represented the apparatus used in kindling fire, and thus as the symbol of sacred fire or as a symbol of the sun, denoting its daily rotation. It has also been interpreted as the mystic representation of lightning or of the god of the tempest, or the emblem of the

Aryanpantheon and the primitive Aryan civilization.

Another associated symbol is the ansated cross (ankh or crux ansata) of the ancient Egyptians, often depicted in the hands of the goddess Sekhet, and as a hieroglyphic sign of life or of the living. Egyptian Christians (Copts) adopted it as the emblem of the cross. In his book, The Worship of the Dead, Colonel J. Garnier wrote: "The cross in the form of the 'Crux Ansata' was carried in the hands of the Egyptian priests and Pontiff kings as the symbol of their authority as priests of the Sun god and was called 'the Sign of Life'."

In the Bronze Age a representation of the cross as conceived in Christian art appeared, and the form was popularized. The more precise characterization coincided with a corresponding general change in customs and beliefs. The cross then came into use in various forms on many objects: fibulas, cinctures, earthenware fragments, and on the bottom of drinking vessels. De Mortillet believed that such use of the sign was not merely ornamental, but rather a symbol of consecration, especially in the case of objects pertaining to burial. In the proto-Etruscan cemetery of Golasecca every tomb has a vase with a cross engraved on it. True crosses of more or less artistic design have been found in Tiryns, at Mycenæ, in Crete, and on a fibula from Vulci.

According to W. E. Vine, the cross was used by worshipers of Tammuz, an Ancient Near East deity of Babylonian origin that had the cross-shaped taw (tau) as his symbol.

During the first two centuries of Christianity, the cross may have been rare in Christian iconography, as it depicts a purposely painful and gruesome method of public execution and Christians were reluctant to use it. A symbol similar to the cross, the staurogram, was used to abbreviate the Greek word for cross in very early New Testament manuscripts. The extensive adoption of the cross as Christian iconographic symbol arose from the 4th century.

However, the cross symbol was already associated with Christians in the 2nd century, and by the early 3rd century the cross had become so closely associated with Christ that Clement of Alexandria, who died between 211 and 216, could without fear of ambiguity use the phrase τ□ κυριακ□ν σημε□ον (the Lord's sign) to mean the cross.

The Jewish Encyclopedia states: The cross as a Christian symbol or "seal" came into use at least as early as the second century and the marking of a cross upon the forehead and the chest was regarded as a talisman against the powers of demons. Accordingly the Christian Fathers had to defend themselves, as early as the second century, against the charge of being worshipers of the cross. Christians used to swear by the power of the cross.

The cross is often shown in different shapes and sizes, in many different styles. It may be used in personal jewelry, or used on top of church buildings. It is shown both empty and in crucifix form, that is, with a figure of Christ, often referred to as the corpus (Latin for "body"), affixed to it. Roman Catholic, Anglican and Lutheran depictions of the cross are often crucifixes, in order to emphasize that it is Jesus that is important, rather than the cross in isolation. Large crucifixes are a prominent feature of some Lutheran churches. However, some other Protestant traditions depict the cross without the corpus, interpreting this form as an indication of belief in the resurrection rather than as representing the interval between the death and the resurrection of Jesus.

Crosses are also a prominent feature of Christian cemeteries, either carved on gravestones or as sculpted stelas. Because of this, planting small crosses is sometimes used in countries of Christian culture to mark the site of fatal accidents, or to protest alleged deaths.

In Catholic countries, crosses are often erected on the peaks of prominent mountains, such as the Zugspitze or Mount Royal, so as to be visible over the entire surrounding area.

In contemporary Christianity, the cross is a symbol of the atonement and reminds Christians of God's love in sacrificing his own Son for humanity. It represents Jesus' victory over sin and death, since it is believed that through his death and resurrection he conquered death itself. Colossians 2:15, "Having disarmed the powers and authorities, he made a public spectacle of them, triumphing over them by the cross".

Although Christians accepted that the cross was the gallows on which Jesus died, they had already begun in the 2nd century to use it as a Christian symbol. During the first three centuries of the Christian era the Cross had been "a symbol of minor importance". Martin Luther at the time of the Reformation retained the cross and crucifix in the Lutheran Church. Luther wrote: "The cross alone is our theology." He believed one knows God not through works, but by grace through faith in the work and sufferings of Jesus through the cross."

A closer look at the Old Testament under the Mosaic Law reveals that whoever was found guilty of death was considered cursed of God and hang on a tree. Centuries later, during the Great Roman empire, this mode of punishment was modified and termed crucifixion. It was in this epoch that Jesus lived. His death on the Cross for the sins of humanity was the most demeaning and degrading act, nevertheless it yielded the greatest spiritual rewards for Man, for eternity.

As many as are willing to embrace the Cross appropriate its benefits to the fullest. Notwithstanding, ones approach to the Cross greatly determines God's approach to their cause. A daily journey to the Cross should be an indispensable part of every Christian's life. In this book, I roll out seven things you are bound to experience as a Christian as you daily carry your Cross and follow Christ.

Chapter One

❦

Place of Scorn

Living a Christian life comes with a price tag. On the onset of our salvation, we chose to identify with Christ and His Kingdom, renouncing the old ways and habits, forfeiting our allegiance to the kingdom of darkness and surrendering to the Kingdom of light. We crossed from one spiritual territory to another and since then, everything associated with the dictates and desires of the 'world' are to be mortified on a daily basis. (Colossians 3:5-9) And as citizens of the eternal kingdom, we have taken on a culture and lifestyle reminiscent of our new domain and king. Take a read at Paul's words.

2 Timothy 2:1 *Thou therefore, my son, be strong in the grace that is in Christ Jesus.*

2 Timothy 2:2 *And the things that thou hast heard of me among many witnesses, the same commit thou to faithful men, who shall be able to teach others also.*

2 Timothy 2:3 *Thou therefore endure hardness, as a good soldier of Jesus Christ.*

2 Timothy 2:4 *No man that warreth entangleth himself with the affairs of this life; that he may please him who hath chosen him to be a soldier.*

2 Timothy 2:5 *And if a man also strive for masteries, yet is he not crowned, except he strive lawfully.*

Paul in his later years of life and ministry is writing to Timothy, one of his Son's in the gospel. He is instructing him as a young minister to be strong in the grace of God. In his fatherly letter, he cautions him to remain focused on the spiritual duties and responsibilities that were entrusted to him. He use several examples one of which is having a soldier's mentality and credentials to substantiate his point.

When one enrolls in military service, they swear to uphold and keep the military code; one of which is honoring the uniform and badge they are wearing. Their sole duty is to protect their people, nation and its interests. Being a Soldier is a responsibility that diminishes some of the joys and pleasures that come with civilian life. The liberty to do the things one would have loved to do and go places they would have desired to go to, is sacrificed for the sake of a greater call.

These personnel often find themselves deployed in places out of reach of their homes and families and spend months or years without seeing them; because they are serving their country. Some of the things they get to learn in the process is mental resolve and commitment to an undying cause. Paul in instructing Timothy, drew the analogy of a Christian who has been enrolled as a soldier of Christ. He cautions us to avoid entanglement with the affairs of this world. Those things that cling and entrap us to a point where we are unable to exercise our Christian-soldier-duties like intercession and proclaiming the gospel of Jesus.

Paul also quotes the example of an athlete in a race. Athletes in all fields have a number of things in common. The discipline of training, kind of diet they eat, a good personal trainer and above all, a goal to achieve. These things form the bedrock on which their success is built. They will often times weather the heat or cold of the day, to train hard in order to build endurance, strength and stamina for the anticipated competition. Likewise, as spiritual athletes, we should often embark on the discipline of praying, studying God's word and yielding ourselves to the Holy Spirit who is our guide, helper and personal trainer; with the goal of becoming like Christ and leading others to him.

However, these spiritual disciplines are bound to arouse friction and antagonism with some of your family, friends, work-mates and society. When the folks you used to hang with, do drugs and use foul/cursing language begin seeing a changed and disciplined life of Christ in you, they will brand you a religious fanatic, a loser, moron and on; because they don't understand your transformed life. Others will not stand seeing and being around you. Standing for what is right may earn you laughter, criticism, ridicule and verbal stripping.

Many years ago I walked into my bank to cash a check. I

handed the check to a lady behind the teller and as usual waited on her to hand me the money worth my check. I was surprised when she gave me ten times more than what was expected. I got confused. Counted the money two more times and within my heart I thought, 'is this a mistake or some kind of bonus'. By then, there was a long queue behind me. My conscience said, it must be a mistake on her part. I told the lady, Mum, you have given me more money than the check requires of me. When she cross referenced the check against the amount, her eyes got teary, her hands began shaking, then she muttered to me in a humble, honest and shocked tone, 'thank you Sir, you can't imagine what this has meant to me. Your act of sincerity has helped keep my job and record'. Meanwhile, some of the folks who were in the queue had noticed what was ongoing and I overheard one mumble, 'this fellow is a fool, he has blown the one chance he had to make additional money'. My simple response was, 'I'm a born again Christian.'

There are also seasons and places God allows us to go through that conjure scorn and criticism. I live in Uganda, a country I am so proud of and dearly love. Like New York City, our main City of Kampala is always buzzing with activity; from the car traffic on the roads and throngs of pedestrians moving on the side-walks, to the distant music echoing from the business district. Driving through our City requires patience, restraint and some bit of skill. On a daily basis, I encounter more of the taxi cubs drivers because of their nature of work and business. Some or many of them are mean, cold hearted and full of cursing and are often reckless in their driving. When they are in wrong and you try to speak out, its usual for them to lash out by publicly ridiculing you. I do have a bumper sticker on my car that says, 'JESUS' and many a time I try to exercise restraint and speak to them lovingly that what you are doing or have done is wrong. For the most part, the advise isn't well taken.

Friends, we live in a world that is selfish, mean and ungrateful. Exemplifying the life and personality of Christ comes at a cost. Your attitude and demeanor during such like episodes should be like that of your fore-runner Christ.

When we follow the proceedings that ensued while Jesus was on the cross, we learn about the Art of silence. Silence if rightly employed, can be a great tool. It demonstrates maturity, composure and discipline and can avert, calm and bring to an end scenarios that would have culminated into chaos. Be it domestic or office related. The moments Jesus was being ridiculed on the cross were very delicate. He had all the right to scream back in self defense to his nemeses, yet he resorted to silence. Choosing to absorb the criticism because he knew a Christian life isn't measured by people's praises and plaudits but by God's commendation. At the end He was the victor because through his obedience, he conquered death and the grave. He had reason to say, 'if they hated me, they will also hate you'. Friend, these seasons are an integral part of our Christian life and should never come as a surprise to us. Your citizenship is now in heaven but you are God's ambassador on earth. You answer to the divine King, that is why you may often be misunderstood. Always anticipate the best from people but prepare for the worst. Never expect them to always love and side with you. Persecution comes in different packs.

Mathew 27:37 *And set up over his head his accusation written, THIS IS JESUS THE KING OF THE JEWS.*

Mathew 27:38 *Then were there two thieves crucified*

with him, one on the right hand, and another on the left.

Mathew 27:39 *And they that passed by reviled him, wagging their heads,*

Mat 27:40 *And saying, Thou that destroyest the temple, and buildest it in three days, save thyself. If thou be the Son of God, come down from the cross.*

Mathew 27:41 *Likewise also the chief priests mocking him, with the scribes and elders, said,*

Mathew 27:42 *He saved others; himself he cannot save. If he be the King of Israel, let him now come down from the cross, and we will believe him.*

Mathew 27:43 *He trusted in God; let him deliver him now, if he will have him: for he said, I am the Son of God.*

Mathew 27:44 *The thieves also, which were crucified with him, cast the same in his teeth.*

Chapter Two

❦

Place of (Godly) Sorrow;

When Jesus was leaving earth after his three and a half year assignment, there was a set of marching orders and remarks he left with his disciples. One particular episode that resonates with me in this chapter is what He tells Peter before His arrest and Peter's aftermath actions. Jesus said in Luke 22:32, *"when you have turned again, strengthen your brothers.'* (ESV) The night of His apprehension, Peter went through a defining moment of his life and ministry. His denial of the knowledge of Christ and subsequent penitence, underscores what a life of the Cross should mean to a Christian.

As long as you and I are still clothed in our human-suit, we are bound to transgress, stumble and fall; in our thoughts, words and deeds. God made provision for our daily shortfalls through the blood of His Cross when He said, 'My little children, these things write I unto you, that ye sin not. And if any man sin, we have an advocate with the Father, Jesus Christ the righteous: And he is the propitiation for our sins: and not for ours only, but also for the sins of the whole world. (1 John 2:1-2☐ KJV)'.

The Christian life is a pilgrim's journey with deterrents, traps, roadblocks, hurdles, and on. These are meant to impede our purpose and cause us to jump ship. When we decide to stick to the chase and pursue our highest call, we experience numerous temptations and trials some of which overwhelm us, others rattling us to point of abdication. Notwithstanding, His grace is always sufficient and strength made perfect in our weakness. The seasons we fail are a memento of our unworthiness and they underscore the need of the cleansing Blood of Christ.

They are also a profound reminder of God's unfailing love and mercy demonstrated on the Cross, when He became our perfect substitute, paying the ultimate price we could never have paid given our sinful Adamic nature. This should provoke the godly sorrow for our transgressions and shortfalls in life instead of concealing and branding them as normal, fashionable, trendy and modern. Society through time has adopted fashionable words like, cheating instead of adultery/fornication, helping oneself with another's property instead stealing, under the table deals instead of corruption or bribery, to mention but a few. The Truth will always remain Truth no matter how it is mis-branded or packaged. A set of people catch my eye in this bible text.

Mark 15:39 *And when the centurion, which stood over against him, saw that he so cried out, and gave up the ghost, he said, Truly this man was the Son of God.*

Luke 23:48 *And all the people that came together to that sight, beholding the things which were done, smote their breasts, and returned.*

We glean considerable truth from the happenings of the day Jesus' lifeless body hang on the Cross after a bout of hunger, physical and emotional battering coupled with dehydration from the unrelenting heat of the Middle East. We are told of a centurion who was tasked to oversee His execution. He supervised the proceedings to the letter as he occupied a front seat. Finally when Jesus' assignment was complete, He cried out and let go of his spirit. This soldier, who had faithfully discharged his duties, on seeing what had happened, exclaimed, 'surely this was a righteous man'. (Luke 23:47). Similarly, there were some onlookers and bystanders who through the years had interacted, seen and heard this renown Prophet, Rabbi and Miracle worker. It was no secret in town. The whole of Jerusalem was buzzing with the news of his arrest and pending crucifixion. They had come to witness firsthand his execution. On seeing the manner of death, they were muzzled and horrified. Its gruesome nature moved them to thump their chests in sorrow and pain and leave. Both actions of the centurion and crowd were sympathetic towards the man Jesus but not empathetic. The actions were more outward than inward. These persons totally misread and incorrectly interpreted the 'script'.

The whole idea of the Father sending His Son, Jesus, to die on the cross was the salvation of Man. As a perfect and sinless being, He had no need to trudge the hill to Calvary. But when through His eyes of mercy saw the bondage of Man and eternal banishment, opted to strip himself of glory, take on the form of Man and plead in the Divine court of Justice, guilty of all sins of Man. And after divine justice had been dispensed, He cried, 'It is finished'. (John 19:30)

Contrary to the centurion and standby crowd, the panorama of the Cross is meant to imprint in our spirits a godly kind of sorrow that moves us to thump our chests in penitence for our sin and ask for God's mercy and grace; mindful of the fact that, it was you and I who were supposed to be on that 'tree'. A life of the Cross should teach us to live 'broken-lives'. When we find ourselves in breach of His Word and are willing to break down and admit our shortcomings, we will draw from the healing streams of mercy and grace that freely flow from the Cross.

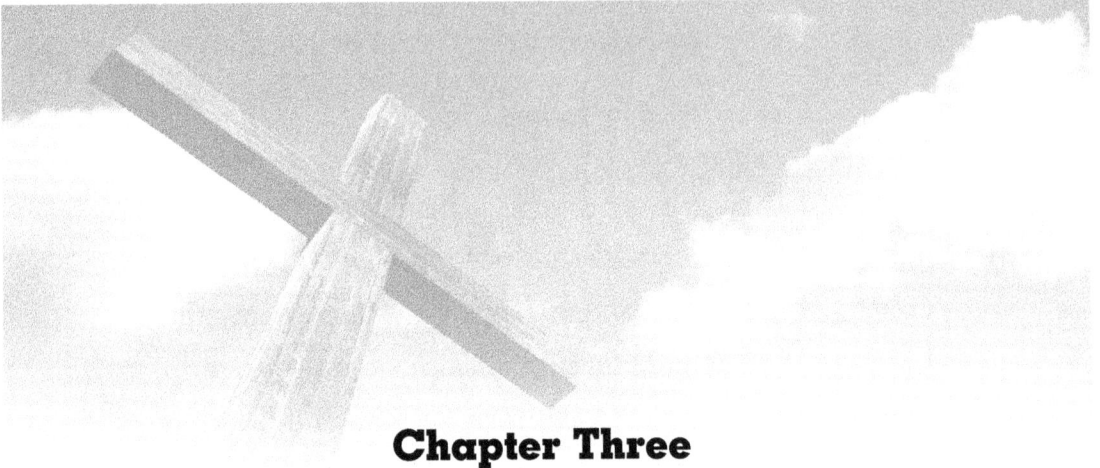

Chapter Three

❦

Place of Sanctification;

The word sanctification in the Bible has to do with cleansing and setting apart. From the Old to the New Testament, when God was calling and setting apart persons for His purpose, a process of cleansing was undergone. In the case of Abraham, it was circumcision. Under the Mosaic Law, animal sacrifices were performed to set apart Levitical priests, Nazarites and other persons who voluntarily offered themselves or were divinely called for service. One particular episode in the New Testament fascinates me. Paul was intercepted by God on his way to Damascus to persecute the Christians there and spent three days of separation and soul searching. When the days were ended, God commissioned him to his lost brethren and gentile nations. Ideally, there is no sanctification that does not entail heart preparation and cleansing.

As Christians, God calls us as a kingdom of kings and priests. As kings, we co-reign with him by dispensing His rule and authority on the earth realm. Sometimes the areas of our rulership are so spiritually demanding that they usurp our spiritual energy and if we are not adequately prepared, there may be a negative flow of energy from them. Notwithstanding, no matter the challenges, our kingly attributes should be similar to those of our great King. And as priests, we serve Him through the offerings and gifts of our prayers, praises and giving. These responsibilities require of us to frequent the Cross, a place where His blood is openly dispensed. When here, we find ourselves hemmed in that place of sanctification because as priests, he constantly requires of us to have our spiritual garments worthy of service. And as kings, we leave renewed and refreshed with new marching orders. A negative mind will perceive a daily visit to the Cross as a guilt-trip instead of a continuous journey of self examination. We cannot be God's priests entrusted to minister to Him and His people (our families, churches, cities and nations) through our worship and intercessions, if we haven't learnt the art of sanctification (dedication).

The devil also through your lifetime will keep casting his darts/arrows at you; via your mind, friends, circumstances and society to cause you to lose focus and grip on life by sulking, grumbling, complaining and doubting. This may eventually pollute your priestly garment and dishonor your Kingly office. We should therefore purpose to live a life of sanctification through self examination because the moment we are sincere with ourselves, God begins the work of transformation in us.

Luke 23:39 *And one of the malefactors which were hanged railed on him, saying, If thou be Christ, save thyself and us.*

Luke 23:40 *But the other answering rebuked him, saying, Dost not thou fear God, seeing thou art in the same condemnation?*

Luke 23:41 *And we indeed justly; for we receive the due*

reward of our deeds: but this man hath done nothing amiss.

Luke 23:42 *And he said unto Jesus, Lord, remember me when thou comest into thy kingdom.*

Luke 23:43 *And Jesus said unto him, Verily I say unto thee, Today shalt thou be with me in paradise.*

We are at a point when the day is far spent and Jesus is hanging on the Cross. The physical, mental and emotionally exhaustion was overwhelming as he carried the whole weight of Man's sin on Him. He would have savored to use the remaining time on that Cross in silence; to rest his body that was screaming with pain and pressure from the long rusty nails and crown of thorns fastened on his head. But amidst the chants and seemingly distant noises of the crowd that were instigated by the priests, an argument ensued. A row broke out between the two thieves crucified on his left and right side. The squabble was about why the so-called Christ wasn't saving them from this predicament. I am surprised that even at this stage of his life, at a point of no return, one of the thieves is still playing the blame game and expecting others to atone for his actions. Perhaps he used to get out of jail free cards from friends and had taken it for granted. He didn't realize that this time, it wasn't business as usual. His luck had run out. He had used his last deck of cards and justice was taking its toll on him. The lashes and scourging he used to get were nothing in comparison to the crucifixion experience.

His fellow interrupted his hoarse and squeaky tone of a voice. Appalled at the ridiculous comments emanating from his mouth, -hushes him saying, 'don't you fear God'? We have received the due reward of our deeds but this man has done nothing wrong'. He then directs his conversation to Jesus and says, 'Lord, remember me when you come into your Kingdom'. (Luke23:41-42). Two things happened at this instant; one is the acknowledging of his sins and the other imploring Jesus to accept him into His Kingdom. Notice the way he addressed Him, calling him Lord. Interpreted from Greek, the word means, 'Supreme in authority, Controller and Master'. A radical change took place in the life of this thief that caused his life to turn around forever. At the very point of death, when everyone had written him off and closed his life's journal, a new life unfolded occasioned by a willingness to admit his mistakes and know there is a greater one.

As Christians, there is a life's lesson gleaned from this text. There will always be a set of people. One that justify themselves, unwilling to confess and come to terms with their status AND the ones who tire of running, are hemmed in with circumstances and are at a point of abdication. To the latter, there is always a way out. The Cross is the place we run to knowing that we can identify with the Christ-man who carried ALL our sins and failures. Here, we willingly ventilate what is on our heart and allow Him be Lord of our lives. When we do, He justifies and sanctifies us by his blood and 'refreshes' our kingdom status.

Chapter Four

❦

Place of Separation

God's dealings with his people have/will always be a mystery. From the Old Testament Bible Patriarchs and early Church folk to the present day Christian. When he hand-picks us as His own, and for his purpose, he takes us through seasons of testing and maturity that reveal byproducts of tears and joy.

In Exodus 2:11-3:15, we learn of Moses, one of God's greatest generals. At the age of forty, Moses had a hunch he had been called to be a deliverer of God's people from Egypt. One morning he takes it upon himself to be judge and executioner of an Egyptian who was mistreating a Hebrew slave. He kills and buries him somewhere in the sand. His deed didn't go unnoticed, the next day he tries to arbitrate between two Hebrew men fighting, but is derided and called a murderer by one of them. Realizing that his act of murder was common knowledge, flees for his life out of Egypt into Midian where he ends up in the house of Jethro, a Priest of Midian. While here, he begins a new life, marries one of Jethro's daughters and takes on a nomadic job of looking after his Father in Law's flock. Years flesh by, he has two sons and the memory of Egypt is faded from his mind.

One morning as he is going about his daily chores, chooses to lead the flock to the back side of the desert, around Mount Horeb. Little does he know this was going to be a defining moment in his life and carrier.

He sees a bush that is burning but isn't consumed. Curiosity moves him to draw closer and when he does, hears a voice beckoning and instructing him to remove his shoes; because of the sanctity of the place. At some point during this encounter, God dealt with Moses on a personal level, his attitude and temperament that could have been occasioned by his natural weakness of stammering.

This kind of separation bears resemblance to a Christian's daily journey to the Cross. A place we go to in seclusion of prayer, self_-examination and fellowship with God; as He gets to work on us. There are areas in your life (destiny, family, ministry, career) that require a closed in session with the Master.

Peter was one of Jesus' most trusted followers. He hung around him for over three years, accompanied him on several interstate travels and saw the diverse and overwhelming miracles performed on those that were dead and diseased. He was privileged to be part of the inner circle that had access to the inner secrets of its Master. He even ran some special errands for Jesus. Yet on the fateful day Jesus was apprehended, he ostentatiously denied knowledge of him not once or twice.

At that instant, Peter's life took on a major twist. Seeing the words Jesus had spoken to him some hours back being fulfilled, storms out of the courtyard. Fearful and guilt ridden, he finds a spot where he unceasingly began to sob. This must have gone on for hours, realizing he had openly denied the one person he had blatantly told, 'though others abandon you, I will never'. As moments fleshed by, I can only imagine that there was intense heart searching within him. In one part of his mind, it's possible that the devil was whispering, 'it is over you can never be forgiven', yet in another part of his mind, Peter could possibly be hearing-, the words of Jesus resonating, 'when you have turned again, strengthen your brothers' (ESV). He chose to follow the words of His master, and in deep repentance, made a turn around.

Friends, we are bound to encounter similar seasons in our lives. The packaging may differ with persons and circumstances. There are those areas we 'deny' our master through our confession, unbelief, attitude, thoughts and deeds. These scenarios often pop up when we are against a wall OR have hit rock bottom. On the flip side, these are the times God is beckoning and needs our attention. Unless you and I realize that these sessions are an integral part of our lives, we will end up missing their benefits.

The best example is starring at us in the text below. Jesus has done His part and it is a couple of hours before He lets go of His spirit in the Father's hands. We will NEVER comprehend the 'tension' that was going on in His mind and spirit. A perfect being, God in the flesh, never once separate from fellowship with His Father, now hangs on this brutal cross with not a word from His loving Father. I can imagine that The hours seemed like forever as a thick darkness, filled with eerie creatures shouted, scolded and did spite him; voices only His spiritual ear could make out. This moment of separation is what redefined the destiny of the human race. His obedience unto death is the reason you and I have the blessed assurance of Eternal security. Jesus chose to make His time of separation count. Will you?

Mathew 27:45 *Now from the sixth hour there was darkness over all the land unto the ninth hour.*

Mathew 27:46 *And about the ninth hour Jesus cried with a loud voice, saying, Eli, Eli, lama sabachthani? that is to say, My God, my God, why hast thou forsaken me?*

Chapter Five

❦

Place of Substitution;

In the Old Covenant system, a special goat was set aside as a substitute for the sins of the people. On it, the high priest confessed the sins of the nation and it was released into the wilderness where it wandered till it died or was eaten by wild beasts. In the New Testament dispensation, Jesus was the perfect substitute, the lamb of God that took our place of condemnation and death. He became vicariously liable for all our sins on that Cross. The principle of substitution has remained etched in the Cross. It depends on the way it is appropriated.

The Cross is the perfect altar we lay the things that friends, foes and society do to us. Heartaches, disappointments, frustrations, abuse, divorce, defamation, separation, rejection, child and spousal abuse are among the many and 'nasty' things life throws at us. Quick fixes like revenge and suicide have only exacerbated situations leaving us in a perpetual state of regret. Others have employed the non_-active form of revenge by exhibiting intense anger, resentment, bitterness, un-forgiveness, isolation and depression. These are poisons that slowly and systematically eat into the life of its recipient; till they pine away. Life doesn't discriminate between young and old, rich or poor, hispanic or oriental, black or white, atheist or Christian. It will try to bury you. The option of circumventing its traps is yours. However, in the big equation of life, God has made primary provision for all humanity through the Cross.

When you prefer this narrow path to the ones that offer seeming ease and sensual satisfaction, you will reap what is divine and fulfilling. With no other place to run that will cater for the deep seated issues of your heart, the Cross stands out as the sublime effigy that calls out to as many as can, to come and relinquish their pain, frustrations, bitterness and burdens. It is imbued with unceasing power that flows from it to its respondents.

Many have flocked and are still making their way to this place of sanctity. No genuine seeker has ever been turned away. God made sufficient provision for as few as one person to as many as all humanity to stand in this place and be served. It is not one of personal preference or partiality. The only protocol is humility and honestly. A place where the door is always open and the helpline active 24 hours a day. One can choose to stay an entire day/night OR spend just a moment. It's no place for the 'busy' or those who are in a rush.

In this perfect environment, awash with God's grace, goodness and mercy, we begin ventilating and offloading the weights of life. To use the computing language, we uninstall those dangerous files-, life installed onto our life's hard-drive. These are the reason our spiritual and emotional system had slowed down or crushed. Afterwards, we endeavor to install the good files; peace, joy, forgives, love, patience, self-control, kindness, humility and so on—that will help boost our 'system' and restore our life-component.

As a pastor and traveling missionary, I have been

privileged to witness, interact and hear amazing testimonies of people whose lives were turned around. From stories of contemplated suicides, planned revenge and denouncing Jesus, to spiritual recommitments, revitalized marriages and folks embracing a kingdom life of victory. The Christian journey should be lived as an exchange life. It is punctuated with deposits and withdraws. In the accounting language, it is a system of double entry, with debits and credits. However, for every debit, there should be a corresponding credit. In simple terms, when you decide to empty, you should make effort to fill the blank spot. It is a consistent pattern of life.

A while ago, scientists discovered one the many values of sleep and why after we awake we,- are refreshed and ready to go about our days work. They found out that in the course of our sleep, the brain goes to work by flashing out the poisonous and dangerous neurons that have accumulated in the brain during the day. Only the inventor of this 'sleep thing' figured out this equation and can provide the details. Now if you are the type that intentionally robs yourself of your sleep time, you are missing out with this wonderful exchange. When you allow your body to rest through sleep, you will reap the benefits of its cleansing process.

I always like running back to our best example to substantiate my points. When we read Luke 23:26-43 and the other Gospel accounts of the crucifixion, there was an ongoing fracas at the base of the Cross. A couple of Roman soldiers were raffling over Jesus' garment seeing it couldn't be divided. While in the immediate vicinity, others were taunting him based on the inscription that was written, 'King of the Jews'. All this plethora of behavior would have occasioned disgust and despondence on His part, but Jesus knew too well that he was at the place of substitution. The right course of action was forgiveness. First of all, his accusers and crucifiers were ignorant of this spiritual mystery and eternal plan of redemption. They were naïve participants in this bizarre unfolding of events. To vent His anger and frustration on them, would jeopardize the entire salvation mission. However, what was hurting was, the people he had been sent to save, had turned their backs on him. Notwithstanding, in calm resolve of mind and spirit, He exchanged love for hate and forgiveness for bigotry. This is the attribute our King and Lord left us to follow. It's when we are hurt most that we forgive most. It's a principle of quality versus quantity. Choose to make the Cross a place of substitution. And as a good steward of the gift of life you have been entrusted with, learn to often do some stock taking. Getting rid of the old, expired and harmful 'stock' AND re-stock yourself with those 'fresh and healthy products' that will make your life count.

Luke 23:33 *And when they were come to the place, which is called Calvary, there they crucified him, and the malefactors, one on the right hand, and the other on the left.*

Luke 23:34 *Then said Jesus, Father, forgive them; for they know not what they do. And they parted his raiment, and cast lots.*

Chapter Six

Place of Surrender;

Surrender is a term I first heard of in the movies when I was young. While watching movies about the first and second world war, I could see prisoners of war being led captive by their captors. In some cases, the prisoners were shot dead on the spot, while others with their hands raised as a sign of surrender, yielded their authority and power to their captors. At that time, I could not fully make out the significance of their act. Some years later, I could better relate to the occurrence because it was happening in my back yard. The internal political wars and conflicts that rocked my country in the 1980's were often showcased by pictures/video clips on our television sets; as rebel soldiers surrendered to the government forces. The word surrender took on new meaning when I saw the rebel-soldiers act of abdication and their captors treatment.

Wen I gave my life to Jesus, the word, surrender, took on true meaning. After living in and being associated with the kingdom of evil, because the devil is the prince of darkness and god of this world; I denounced his kingdom, became a Christian and surrendered my allegiance to the Kingdom of light and its King. I, like every other defector (better said-Christian convert), turned my back on the old master—the devil AND swore allegiance to my new Master-Jesus all the days of my life. Like every professing Christian, this automatically made me a Citizen of the Kingdom of God with all rights and privileges of a child of God.

However, this my friend, was only a start of this journey. As long as you and I are still on earth the Kingdom of darkness will do everything possible to steal, kill and destroy us. This is the threefold mission of our age long adversary, to cause us to defect to his kingdom OR cause us to live a stressful life in the Kingdom of God.

The key to upholding our citizenship is living a life of continuous surrender. Being a Christian and Citizen of the Kingdom of God doesn't absolve you from attacks. Remember you are a defector and all through your pilgrimage on this realm, will be attacked and resisted. The place of the (Cross)you once visited and transformed your life, now becomes one of frequency. It is here that the vows once made are always renewed. The more you visit this spot, the more you realize your need of surrender. While here, you come to terms with yourself by letting go and entrusting God with everything that relates to your life.-The Cross teaches us that the only way to embrace a higher level is ceasing to struggle and to just surrender.

Abraham lived through out his life waiting and trusting God for a son of promise. He had his share of mistakes, having a son through Hagar, a house mistress, and going to Egypt and lying to Abimelech the King that Sarah was his sister. Yet his tenacious faith in God brought the rewards of the long awaited son—Isaac at a ripe age of 100 years.

The season of joy soon ebbed when God awakened and required him to sacrifice his only son Isaac. In those moments, Abraham must have had a thousand questions jostling through his mind, but his act of obedience evidenced by his three-day journey to Mount Moriah, said it all. The trip may have been the longest and worrisome of his entire life yet he didn't question a divine command. When he reached the spot of sacrifice, he laid the wood in order, Isaac on the altar and stretched his hand to slay the boy. A voice bellowed from above stopping him from his enterprise and the rest is history. Friends, we wouldn't have known about this great patriarch and his achievement if he hadn't demonstrated such obedience and surrender to God. Abraham graduated to being a father of faith to us all because he understood the meaning of surrender.

The life of Jesus will always be our bench mark. His surrender to God led him to let go of His spirit to create an opening for Him into another dimension. The moment Jesus chose to strip Himself of glory and be clothed in flesh and blood, was when the plan of redemption was set in motion. For thirty three years on earth, He prepared Himself for the time He would be the sacrificial lamb. During His years on earth, He revealed the love and mercy of His father to countless folk as He; brought hope to the lost, mended broken hearts, healed the sick and demonstrated to humanity and the kingdom of darkness that God is sovereign and supreme. However, the only way (divinely ordained) He would step into another realm was to surrender His life to the point of death. This act would make Him the author of eternal salvation, the first born from the dead and our Eternal High Priest. His name would be given overwhelming status in heaven above, on the earth and in the lowest parts of the earth (Hades), so that, at its mention every knee should bow and every tongue confess that He is Lord. The only way up was down. The seed had to die for the fruit to manifest. That day's events can be best summed in this text.

Luke 23:45 *And the sun was darkened, and the veil of the temple was rent in the midst.*

Luke 23:46 *And when Jesus had cried with a loud voice, he said, Father, into thy hands I commend my spirit: and having said thus, he gave up the ghost.*

God will often times give us sneak peeks into our future.

Maybe you have received a dream or heard an inspiring sermon that the Lord spoke to you about your future and you believe it and become excited, this is God giving you a sneak peak of your future. However, between your now and future, there will places of surrender to visit. Those higher levels and dimensions you aspire for aren't going to come to you like 'Santa Claus on a reindeer' OR like a tooth-fairy. They will often involve wrestling bouts with God like Jacob did the night he was left alone; (Genesis 32:22-32). These 'matches' will drain and empty us of our pride, arrogance and mentality, leaving us broken and ready for the Master's use. Then and only then will He qualify us for the great doors and opportunities that we have so much savored. Are you willing and ready for the adventure?

Chapter Seven

❦

Place of Salvation;

Ever stopped for a moment, sat back on your recliner and wondered why God is called the Alpha and Omega, Author and Finisher, the Beginning and End? Well, one good reason is that whatever He starts, he completes. Our God is a finisher! The story of creation is one of the greatest events ever been documented. For five days, God goes to work as He speaks the heavens and the earth into being. He devotes the sixth day to fashioning Man in His image and likeness, and on the seventh day when He is done with his 'creation-assignment' gets to rest. Not only was He done, but what He tasked Himself to do, was perfect. Of course there was no one to vet or evaluate His work, so He commended Himself. Genesis 1:31 And God saw everything that he had made, and, behold, it was very good. And the evening and the morning were the sixth day.

And through the eon of time, in the Holy Scriptures, we see His finger on nations, individuals and events; shaping and defining their destinies. From the journey of the children of Israel out of Egypt till they are settled in the land of Canaan, to raising a ruddy and insignificant shepherd boy to become one of the greatest kings of Israel. He took a young Hebrew dreamer and made him one of the finest Statesmen of his time in a foreign land AND turned the latter years of Job's life into an overflowing joy. I can go on and on rehearsing God's finishing touches on what He sets His hand to do.

However, His chronicles would be incomplete if the redemption story was omitted. The -idea of redemption was with God from the beginning of time because He knew that Man (Adam) would relinquish his authority and inheritance of earth to Satan. Permit my jargon, God had a Plan B for Man's restitution, which was really "Plan A". Revelation 13:8 Everyone living on earth will worship it, everyone whose name is not written in the Book of

Life. That book belongs to the lamb who was slaughtered before the creation of the world. (God's Word Translation Bible).

It was only a matter of time till this plan would be unveiled. Our Heavenly Father being a methodical God, works through seasons and times. When the time was ripe, the Word of God, as He was/is called in Heaven, stepped out of eternity into time and set the redemption clock into motion. His journey to the hill of Calvary, bearing the Cross, was the only way this story could be written. It is at Golgotha that Man's history was re-written and his destiny forever changed.

The introductory pages of this book give us an overview of the Cross, its history, why and how it stands out as a Christian emblem. Christianity derives its foundation and significance in the Cross of Christ. It is an indispensable part of our lives.

The Cross is the intersection between our past life and future. It is our place of salvation. Translated from Greek, the word 'salvation' means, deliverance of spirit, soul and body. It encapsulates the three aspects of our human existence. When we confessed the Lordship of Jesus, our spirits were liberated (redeemed). Our physical and emotional health was also catered for but because we still live in a human body and possess a soul, there remains work to be done. That is why they are often a target of the devil. He always tries to inflict sickness, disease, pain, anxiety, worry, fear, destruction and death. Notwithstanding, if we discover the inherent power in the Cross and become genuine seekers that make daily pit-stops at it, we shall reap its rewards and become guaranteed receivers.

When Jesus cried, 'It is finished', (John 19:30) every affair regarding Man was fittingly addressed. The sacrifice of His body was duly accepted by the Father. The transaction was completed and the veil of separation that lingered for ages between a Holy God and fallen Man was forever torn down through Jesus' flesh. There is now unlimited access to God by a repentant sinner reaching out for mercy and forgiveness AND a Child of God running to his/her loving Father. At this rendezvous, the Cross, the total salvation package was discharged;

spiritual, financial, emotional, physical, marital and on. Everything pertaining to this life and the one after was taken care of.

At the Cross many earthly and eternal rewards have been secured by countless Christians. From the first century saint that endured gross torture and persecution from ruthless Roman emperors to the present day Christian experiencing the saving grace and goodness of Christ. For many of these early Christians, awe-inspiring acts of divine justice and justification were demonstrated; kingdoms being conquered on their behalf, mouths of lions shut, miraculously escaping death, finding strength in moments of weakness, were made powerful in battle, women received their loved ones back from the dead; all because of the power of the Cross at work in them.

Living in a generation where technology has reduced the world into a global village, one is able to witness and hear amazing and countless stories of God's supernatural provision, healing and divine encounters. Jesus is still the same yesterday, today and forever. The power of the Cross has never diminished but is constantly exerting its influence on its pursuant. The Cross is the voice that echoes in our conscience because it bears the print of the spotless blood of the Christ. It is this blood that speaks better promises. Hebrews 12:24 You have come to Jesus, who arranged the new covenant, and to the sprinkled blood that promises much better things than does the blood of Abel. (Good News Bible).

The Book of Hebrews instructs us to look to Jesus the author and finisher of our faith. Deciding to focus on and be motivated by the joy that was set before Him, HE ENDURED THE CROSS, despised the shame (torture, scorn and betrayal) and is now set down at the right hand of His majesty-. (Hebrews 12:1-3). His endurance was driven by His immediate neighbor, one of the repentant sinners on a cross AND the millions upon millions that he envisioned in eternity future singing the song of the Lamb. He opted to 'road-test' the efficiency of the Cross with His own life, and the results yielded fruit on the spot. This was a massive boost to all His followers knowing that, the Cross carries a life time warranty of rewards both in this life and the one after. At the Cross, everything about you and me was finished before our lives ever began. I pray your perspective of this great masterpiece will radically change, as you begin to patiently anticipate its returns. The prerequisite is, endeavoring to make it your daily refueling station.

Luke 23:42 *And he said unto Jesus, Lord, remember me when thou comest into thy kingdom.*

Luke 23:43 *And Jesus said unto him, Verily I say unto thee, Today shalt thou be with me in paradise.*

John 19:28 *After this, Jesus knowing that all things were now accomplished, that the scripture might be fulfilled, saith, I thirst.*

John 19:29 *Now there was set a vessel full of vinegar: and they filled a sponge with vinegar, and put it upon hyssop, and put it to his mouth.*

John 19:30 *When Jesus therefore had received the vinegar, he said, It is finished: and he bowed his head, and gave up the ghost.*

Conclusion

From the opening chapters to the last pages of this book, we have seen how multi-faceted the Cross is. This divine insignia that will forever be etched in the minds of God's redeemed, resonates with purpose and power. The book of revelation hints on the song of the Lamb we, the redeemed,- shall forever be singing. However, it doesn't give us details about the stanzas or chorus to the song; but a hunch tells me, the words of the Cross will be incorporated.

We live in a human society where bigotry prevails. Unfortunately, it is a way of life in this world. There are those that will accept you and others will not. Some people only favor folks within their social, political and economic circles. The Christian who has painfully attained a good future from a humble background, with few or none to piggy back on, can only merit their achievement to God's mercy and grace. I, like many others, would not be where I am, if it was not God's love and compassion showcased on the Cross. I didn't have to pay colossal sums of money or please anyone to access it. Irrespective of ones race, gender, age and status, there will always be room at the Cross. It is the one place that has never run out of room for a seeker. It always stands out beckoning in the stillness of the night and busy schedule of the day, 'the message of the cross is foolishness to those who are perishing but unto us who are being saved, it is the power of God'.- (1 Corinthians 1:18). It's a one stop for a heart that chooses to offload and replenish. Its your call. You can get the best out of it.

Luke 14:26 *You cannot be my disciple, unless you love me more than you love your father and mother, your wife and children, and your brothers and sisters. You cannot come with me unless you love me more than you love your own life.*

Luke 14:27 *You cannot be my disciple unless you carry your own cross and come with me. (Contemporary English Version).*

Other Books written by Andrew Allans Mutambo:

1. Four Faces of a Worshipper.

2. Worship Keys for Worth-full Living.

3. Gates of Worship.

4. Purpose of praise.

5. Principles of Faith.

6. Dynamics of God's Word.

Coming Soon:

1. Seven Operations of Faith.

2. Seven Characteristics of Prayer.

3. Nine Elements of Worship.

4. Composition of Worship.

5. Seven Locks of the Anointing.

References:

1. Christianity: an introduction by Alister E. McGrath 2006 ISBN 1-4051-0901-7 pages 321-323 [1]

2. Marucchi, Orazio. "Archæology of the Cross and Crucifix." The Catholic Encyclopedia. Vol. 4. New York: Robert Appleton Company, 1908.

3. John Garnier (1904). The worship of the Dead. p. 226. Retrieved 2011-12-10.

4. Vine's Expository Dictionary of New Testament Words, "Cross, Crucify". See, also, Abram Herbert Lewis, Paganism surviving in Christianity, G.P. Putnam's sons, 1892, pp 237, 238.

5. Hutado, Larry (2006). "The staurogram in early Christian manuscripts: the earliest visual reference to the crucified Jesus?". In Kraus, Thomas. New Testament Manuscripts. Leiden: Brill. pp. 207–26. ISBN 978-90-04-14945-8.

6. Stranger, James (2007). "Archeological evidence of Jewish believers?". In Skarsaune, Oskar. Jewish Believers in Jesus The Early Centuries. City: Baker Academic. p. 715. ISBN 9780801047688.

7. ""Octavius"". Ccel.org. 2005-06-01. Retrieved 2011-12-10.

8. Minucius Felix speaks of the cross of Jesus in its familiar form, likening it to objects with a crossbeam or to a man with arms outstretched in prayer (Octavius of Minucius Felix, chapter XXIX).

9. "Stromata, book VI, chapter XI". Earlychristianwritings. com. 2006-02-02. Retrieved 2011-12-10.

10. Apology., chapter xvi. In this chapter and elsewhere in the same book, Tertullian clearly distinguishes between a cross and a stake.

11. (De Corona, chapter 3)

12. Stott, John (2006). The Cross of Christ (20th

Anniversary ed.). Downers Grove: InterVarsity Press. p. 27. ISBN 0-8308-3320-X.

13. "Jewish Encyclopedia". Jewish Encyclopedia. Retrieved 2011-12-10., (see Apocalypse of Mary, viii., in James, "Texts and Studies," iii. 118).

14. De Corona, chapter 3, written in 204.

15. Keith Houston, Shady Characters (W. W. Norton & Company 2013 ISBN 978-0-39306442-1), pp. 97 and 106

16. The perhaps 1st-century Epistle of Barnabas sees the letter T as indicating the cross of Christ (Chapter 9, 7)

17. 'Apologia,' xii., xvii., and Minucius Felix, 'Octavius,' xxix" 9 (Jewish Encyclopedia, article "Cross").

18. Jan Willem Drijvers, Helena Augusta: The mother of Constantine the Great and the legend of her finding of the True Cross, Brill 1992, p. 81.

19. Tertullian, Apology., chapter xvi.

20. (Tertullian, De Corona, chapter 3)

21. Martin Luther: Catholic Critical Analysis and Praise

22. Nicholas Ridley, A Treatise on the Worship of Images, written before 1555.

23. James Calfhill, An aunsvvere to the Treatise of the crosse (An answer to John Martiall's Treatise of the cross) at 1565.

24. Theodore Beza, in his Answer to the Colloquium of Montheliard at 1588, according to Jaroslav Pelikan, The Christian Tradition: A History of the Development of Doctrine, Vol. 4, University of Chicago Press 1985, p. 217.

25. Peter Blickle, Macht und Ohnmacht der Bilder.: Reformatorischer Bildersturm im Kontext der europäischen Geschichte, Oldenbourg Verlag, 2002, pp. 253-272.

26. Religious Politics in Post-Reformation England: Essays in Honour of Nicholas Tyacke, Boydell & Brewer, 2006, p. 26.

27. Henry Dana Ward, History of the cross, the pagan origin, and idolatrous adoption and worship of the image, at 1871.

28. Mourant Brock, The cross, heathen and Christian: A fragmentary notice of its early pagan existence and subsequent Christian adoption, London 1879.

29. John Denham Parsons, The non-Christian cross; an enquiry into the origin and history of the symbol eventually adopted as that of our religion, at 1896.

30. David Williams, Deformed Discourse: The function of the Monster in Mediaeval thought and literature, McGill-Queen's Press 1999, p. 161.

31. Christopher R. Fee & David Adams Leeming, Gods, Heroes & Kings: The battle for mythic Britain, Oxford University Press, 2001, p. 113.

32. What Does the Bible Really Teach?. Watch Tower Society. pp. 204–205.

33. New World Translation of the Holy Scriptures, appendix 5C, page 1577

34. Franz 2007, p. 150

35. Riches, by J.F. Rutherford, Watch Tower Bible & Tract Society, 1936, page 27.

36. Hinckley, Gordon B (May 1975). "The Symbol of Christ". Ensign.

37. Hinckley, Gordon B (April 2005). "The Symbol of Our Faith". Ensign.

38. Hunter, Howard W. (November 1994). "Exceeding Great and Precious Promises". Ensign.

39. McKeever, Bill. "Why No Crosses?". Mormonism Research Ministry. Retrieved 1 April 2013.

40. "General Instruction of the Roman Missal, 117" (PDF). Retrieved 2011-12-10.

41. "Cross Crosslet". Seiyaku.com. 2008-11-25. Retrieved 2011-12-10.

42. http://www.nmuc.org/OffCentr.htm accessed on 2012-04-21

43. "Dannebrog" by Hans Christian Bjerg, p.12, ISBN 87-7739-906-4.

44. "NSC NETWORK – Analogical review on Saint Thomas Cross- The symbol of Nasranis-Interpretation of the Inscriptions". Nasrani.net. Retrieved 2011-12-10.